meditation
for
beginners

JACK KORNFIELD

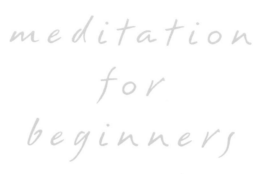

meditation
for
beginners

Six Guided Meditations for Insight, Inner Clarity,
and Cultivating a Compassionate Heart

SOUNDS TRUE

Sounds True, Inc., Boulder, CO 80306
© 2004 Jack Kornfield

Published 2004
Printed in Korea

ISBN 1-59179-148-0

Audio learning programs by Jack Kornfield from Sounds True:

After the Ecstasy, the Laundry

The Beginner's Guide to Buddhism

The Beginner's Guide to Forgiveness

Beginner's Mind (with Sharon Salzberg and Shinzen Young)

Buddhism for Beginners

The Inner Art of Meditation

Meditation for Beginners

Meditations of the Heart

A Path with Heart

The Roots of Buddhist Psychology

Your Buddha Nature

TABLE OF CONTENTS

CHAPTER
ONE

The Ancient Art of Meditation

MEDITATION FOR BEGINNERS offers the central training and teachings found in the best Buddhist monasteries translated for western society. In *Meditation for Beginners*, you will find some of the simplest and most universal of these practices of meditation—in particular, the practices of mindfulness and lovingkindness. An integral part of this instruction will be the six fundamental meditation practices included on the enclosed CD. These guided meditations were recorded at actual meditation retreats and are designed to give you a direct experience of the material presented in this book.

The point of these teachings has nothing to do with becoming a Buddhist, or learning any eastern ceremonies or rituals or bowing. What is important is that you learn how to work with meditation in order to find benefits from it in your life. When we take time to quiet ourselves, every human being can sense that our lives could be lived with greater compassion and greater wakefulness. To meditate is to support this inner potential and allow it to come forth into our lives.

There are many good forms of meditation practice. A good meditation practice is any one that develops awareness or mindfulness of our body and our senses, of our mind and heart. It does not really matter which kind you choose. What is more important is that after you choose a form of meditation you stay with it, and practice it regularly. Meditation takes discipline, just like learning how to play the piano. If you want to learn how to play the piano, it takes more than just a few minutes a day, once in a while, here and there. If you really want to learn any important skill—whether it is playing the piano or meditation—it grows with perseverance, patience, and systematic training.

So pick a type of meditation that appeals to you and practice it. Work with it every day, and work with a teacher if you can, or find circumstances where you can sit together with other people. In the process of practicing regularly, you will begin to develop your capacity to open to the present moment. You will begin to develop patience and compassion when you sit regularly and you will open to everything that is here.

Meditation for Beginners will present the most important basic exercises for mindfulness mediation, also called *vipassana* practice, the heart of Buddhist meditation. Vipassana (a Pali word meaning "to see things as they really are") is the most widely practiced form of meditation in southeast Asia and is central to all Buddhist traditions. This practice emphasizes mindful attention, developing an immediate awareness of one's experience in all spheres of activity.

The meditations in *Meditation for Beginners* are designed to help you shine the light of mindfulness on every aspect of your daily experience—and to show you how to extend the healing power of lovingkindness to yourself and others. Mindfulness practice is also called "insight meditation." It does not seek to focus attention on a meditative image of Buddha, or a deity, or a light, or a candle, or sacred words. Instead, through mindfulness we discover a way to develop a stillness in the midst of activity. Then, even the most mundane, repetitive experiences—such as eating, walking, or answering the phone—can be drawn into the field of meditative awareness, included in the practice of mindfulness. In this way, our meditation is not an exercise that we do every once in a while, but rather a way of being that we can carry with us every moment of our days.

Mindfulness helps train us to be more present and alive for whatever we meet to develop what Alan Watts describes as the art of living: "The art of living...is neither careless drifting on the one hand nor fearful clinging to the past...on the other. It consists in being completely sensitive to each moment, in regarding it as utterly new and unique, in having the mind open and wholly receptive."

To begin to meditate is to look into our lives with interest and kindness and discover how to be wakeful and free. We have so many ideas and beliefs about ourselves. We tell ourselves stories about what we want and who we are, smart or kind. Often these are the unexamined and limited ideas of others that we have internalized and then gone on to live out. To meditate is to discover new possibilities, to awaken the capacity that each of us has to live more wisely, more lovingly, more compassionately, and more fully.

CHAPTER
TWO

Why Meditate?

THERE IS A STORY TOLD about the Buddha shortly after he was enlightened. As he was walking down the dusty road he met a traveler who saw him as a handsome yogi exuding a remarkable energy. The traveler asked him, "You seem very special. What are you? Are you some kind of an angel or deva? You seem unhuman." "No," he said. "Well, are you some kind of god then?" "No," he said. "Well, are you some kind of wizard or magician?" "No," he replied. "Well, are you a man?" "No." "Then what are you?" At this the Buddha answered, "I am awake." In those three words—"I am awake"—he gave the whole of Buddhist teachings. The word "Buddha" means one who is awake. To be a Buddha is to be one who has awakened to the nature of life and death, and awakened and freed our compassion in the midst of this world.

The practice of meditation does not ask us to become a Buddhist or a meditator or a spiritual person. It invites us to fulfill the capacity we each have as humans to awaken. The skill of becoming more mindful, and more present, and more compassionate, and more awake is something we may learn sitting on a meditation cushion, but this capacity for awareness helps in computer programming, playing tennis, lovemaking, or walking by the ocean and listening to life around you. In fact, to awaken, to be really present, is the central art in all other arts.

What is that which we can awaken to? We awaken to what Buddhists call the dharma. "Dharma" is the Sanskrit and Pali word that refers to the universal truths: to the laws of the universe and the teachings that describe it. In this sense, finding the dharma is quite immediate. It is the wisdom that is always present to be discovered.

It is different than waiting for God to come down to us in a cloud of glory, or a big spiritual enlightenment, or a wonderful, otherworldly experience. The dharma of wisdom, what we can awaken to, is the truth that is right where we are when we let go of fantasies and memories and come into the reality of the present. When we do that and pay careful attention, we start to see the characteristics of the dharma in the very life in which we live.

One of the first characteristics of the dharma that shows itself in meditation is impermanence and uncertainty. "Thus shall you think of this fleeting world," it says in one Buddhist sutra. "A star at dawn, a bubble in a stream, a flash of lightning in a summer cloud, an echo, a rainbow, a phantom, and a dream." The more quietly you sit, the more closely you observe, the more you realize that everything you can see is in a state of change. Ordinarily, everything we experience seems solid, including our personality, the world around us, our emotions, and the thoughts in our mind. It is as if we are watching a movie, we can get so caught up in the story until it seems real even though it is actually made of light flickering on a screen. And yet if you focus very carefully on what you are seeing, it is possible to see that the film is actually a series of still pictures, one frame after another. One appears, and then there is a slight gap, and then the next one appears.

The same thing is happening in our lives. Because that is so: nothing in our lives lasts or stays the same for very long. You do not have to be a very adept meditator to see that everything is changing all the time. Have you been able to get any mental states of any kind to last very long? Is there anything in your life that stays the same?

This brings us to dharma's second law. If we want things that are always changing to stay the same and get attached to them, we get disappointed, we suffer. Not because we should suffer—this is not something created to punish us. It is the very way things are, as basic as gravity. If we get attached to something staying the way it is, it does not stop changing. Trying to hold onto "how it was" will only create suffering and disappointment, because life is a river and everything changes.

So when we start to see the laws of nature—that things are impermanent, that attachment causes pain—we can also sense that there must be some other way. And there is. It is the way that can be called "the wisdom of insecurity." This is the ability to flow with the changes, to see everything as a process of change, to relax with uncertainty. Meditation teaches us how to let go, how to stay centered in the midst of change. Once we see that everything is impermanent and ungraspable and that we create a huge amount of suffering if we are attached to things staying the same, we realize that relaxing and letting go is a wiser way to live. We realize that gain and loss, praise and blame, pain and pleasure are part of dance of life, given to each of us born into our human body. Letting go does not mean not caring about things. It means caring for them in a flexible and wise way. In meditation, we pay attention to our body with care and respect.

When we ask, "What is the nature of the body?" we can see that it grows up, it grows old, it gets sick sometimes, and it eventually dies. When we sit to meditate, we can directly feel the state of our body, the tensions we carry, the level of tiredness or energy. Sometimes being in our body feels good, and sometimes it hurts. Sometimes it is quiet, and sometimes it is restless. In meditation we sense that we do not actually own our bodies but rather we just inhabit them for a short time, and during that time they will change by themselves, regardless of what we want to happen. The same is true for our mind and heart, with its hopes and fears, the grief and joy. As we continue to meditate, we learn to relate more wisely to what Zorba the Greek called "the whole catastrophe." Instead of fearing painful experiences and running away from them, or grasping after pleasant experiences hoping that somehow by holding onto them they will last, we come to realize our heart has the capacity to be present for it all, to live more fully and freely where we are. When we realize that everything passes away, not only the good things but the painful things as well, we find a composure in their midst.

So we meditate to awaken to the laws of life. We awaken by shifting the emphasis from so many thoughts and ideas to come into our bodies and our senses. We begin to see how our body and mind operate so that we can come into a wiser relationship with them. The heart of this inner way of practice is mindful listening and careful attention to our environment, to our bodies, to our minds, to our hearts, and to the environment around us. This is what is called mindfulness, a caring and respectful attention.

The mindfulness we train in meditation is helpful everywhere. For instance, you can use it when you are eating. You can hear the voice in your belly that says, "I have had enough, I'm comfortable, I'm nice and full." You can also hear the voice in your tongue when it chimes in, "Gee, but that fruit was so good, let's have a little more." You can hear the eyes when they say, "There is some dessert over there that we haven't tasted yet." And your mother who says, "At least you should finish everything on your plate." With mindfulness, you can learn to hear all of these different voices inside you. You can also learn to listen with full awareness to all of your feelings—to be aware of all of the pleasant and neutral and unpleasant aspects of your experience. You can learn that you do not have to fear that which is painful, and you do not have to grasp for that which is pleasant. We have often been conditioned to believe this is the way, but as we meditate, it quickly becomes apparent that grasping for what is pleasant or fearing things that cause us pain does not lead to peace, and it does not lead to happiness. The truth is that things change whether we want them to or not. Becoming attached to things as they are or pushing things away that we do not like does not stop them from changing. It only leads to further suffering.

Instead, in meditation, we discover a natural, open-hearted, and non-judgmental awareness of our bodies and our feelings. We can gradually bring this kind and open awareness to witness all that's in our minds. We learn to see and trust the law of impermanence—this means that we begin to see the world as it really is. In the midst of it all, we begin to see how we can relate to all of it with compassion, and kindness, and wisdom.

CHAPTER
THREE

The Benefits of Meditation Practice

ONE OF THE MOST BEAUTIFUL IMAGES for meditation I have ever seen is a poster of a smiling Swami Satchidinanda, who was a great Hindu yoga teacher. On this poster he is wearing a little orange loincloth and a long flowing beard, and he is standing balanced on one leg in a classic yoga posture, but he is standing on a surfboard that is coming down on a big wave! Underneath him it says, "You cannot stop the waves, but you can learn to surf." This poster captures the essence of mediation practice: it shows how we can bring mindfulness into the real world, which is full of sensory information, emotions, and change.

Mindfulness meditation does not focus on holding a specific state of mind because in the end you cannot get any state of mind to stay.

Meditation trains us to be present in each moment with awareness, with a greater sense of openness of heart, and with clearer seeing. It can help us learn how to remain more open, and it can help us learn how to love with our whole hearts—and to be unafraid to express that love. Even in our difficulties, meditation can show the possibility of being a little less attached to the inevitable ups and downs in our lives, less afraid of the changes in both pleasures and pains. Meditation helps us to learn to love well, by discovering we can open ourselves to all the aspects of our minds, to whatever is difficult as well as to whatever is easy.

Meditative awareness reduces tension and heals the body. Meditation quiets the mind and gently opens the heart. It steadies the spirit. It helps us learn to live more fully in the reality of the present, to see more clearly the people we live with and the world we live in. As we train in mindfulness, we become more present—so that when we go for a walk in the park, we are not walking among the trees while we are thinking about the bills that we have to pay or our problems at work, something that happened to us yesterday. We can learn to be where we are. Because, basically, being aware in the present moment is the only game in town, and if we miss this moment it will be gone forever.

In this way, meditation can help us fulfill our deepest desires, to discover inner freedom and happiness and to come to a sense of oneness with life. Through it, we come to understand more completely who we are and how to lively wisely in this strange life that we have been born into. The practice helps us to discover what the whole process of life and death is about. And all that is needed is a systematic practice of mindfulness and awareness to foster a sense of inner stillness, so that we can see and learn from everything within and around us.

While it is simple, meditation is not always an easy thing to accomplish. It requires great courage. Carlos Castenada writes about how the Yaqui Indian shaman Don Juan taught him that only a spiritual warrior can withstand the path of knowledge. Only a spiritual warrior never complains or regrets anything. "A spiritual warrior's life is an endless challenge, and challenges cannot possibly be good or bad. The basic difference between an ordinary person and a warrior is that a warrior takes everything as a challenge, while an ordinary person takes everything as a blessing or a curse."

The spirit you will need to bring to meditation is one of openness, of discovery, of seeing. To sit, to walk, and train yourself to bring your attention back to the present moment. To learn how to concentrate mindfully in a balanced way—and to observe your breath, your body, your emotions, and your mind. To learn the patterns of body and mind that cause suffering, and discover release from that suffering. We can also learn how to relate to our lives and the lives of others, with lovingkindness, with a greater sense of understanding and compassion. As he was dying, someone asked Aldous Huxley if he could say what he had learned in all of his work with many spiritual teachers and gurus on his own spiritual journey. Huxley's answer was, "It is embarrassing to tell you this, but it seems to come down mostly to just learning to be kind."

CHAPTER
FOUR

Meditation 1:
Connecting with the Breath

THE PLACE WHERE WE ARE GOING to begin, and where all genuine spiritual practice begins, is by first coming into the body. In this practice, we begin by relating to our breath and our physical body in a mindful, conscious, or wakeful way.

The stilling of your physical body will help a great deal in the quieting of the mind. Your first step, then, is to find a stable and comfortable posture so that you can become aware of your body in the present moment. You can sit squatting on a cushion; you can sit cross-legged; or you can sit on a chair with your feet flat on the floor. What matters is that you have a sense of stability, comfort, and ease. Your body should rest comfortably on the earth as if you are supported by the chair or the cushion, so that you can sit still for a number of minutes without your body being under stress. You should sit relatively straight, with dignity, but without being rigid.

If you are sitting cross-legged, you might want to experiment with making sure that you get your rear end high enough off the floor that your knees can be stable and pointed slightly downwards. You can experiment with different heights to find a way to sit comfortably. Allow your back to be straight enough without being rigid so that your breath can be open and easy and the energy can move through you. Starting with a straight posture also helps to keep you alert. If your posture begins to slump, there is a tendency to go to sleep. Although sleep is wonderful, it is different than meditation.

Once you have found a comfortable posture for sitting straight without being rigid, allow your shoulders to drop and your hands to rest anywhere that is comfortable. People usually rest their hands in their laps or on their knees, which allows the shoulders to be relaxed and the chest to be open and the belly to be soft. You can experiment with your posture in order to find a way to sit where you are upright and at the same time relaxed. To meditate is not to fight with yourself, and if you become uncomfortable—for instance, if there is discomfort in your legs—it is okay to mindfully move them.

Once you have found a comfortable way to sit, then allow your eyes to close gently, or if you want you can leave them open slightly, keep them pointed lightly downward toward the floor and do not look around the room.

Next, bring your awareness into the present moment. Become aware of your environment and the sounds around you. Then become aware of what your body feels like—your physical sensations and perhaps tension within your body. Take a few deep breaths and relax. Then notice the movements of your mind and your feelings—your thoughts, your emotions, your expectations and memories. Now it is time to learn to focus.

For your first meditation, we will use the natural movement of breath to begin to train your awareness to be in the present moment. The first guided meditation included in this set—"Connecting with the Breath"—will help you to become aware of the fact that you are breathing; or more accurately, that breathing is happening.

In meditation, your goal is to experience the breath without directing or changing it, but simply becoming aware of how the breath breathes itself in its own rhythms. Sometimes you will experience your breath as a coolness in the nose or a tingling in the back of your throat, or you may feel the breath more as a movement in your chest, or in the rise and fall of your belly. For the most part, I recommend that you breathe through your nostrils, but if you have a cold or can not breathe through your nose for some reason, you can breathe through your mouth or some combination of the two. Mindfulness meditation is not a breathing exercise like *pranayama* (a yogic form of rapid breathing). It is really an exercise in training your awareness, of being present. So however you feel the breath is okay.

One of the first things you will notice in this meditation is how often the mind wanders off. This is actually the first insight in vipassana meditation, called "seeing the waterfall." You may tell your mind to stay on the breath, but does it listen? Hardly ever. Instead you will catch it planning what you are going to do after you are through meditating, balancing your checkbook, or struggling with your problems. Each time you catch it wandering, you can bring it back to the breath for about three breaths and then it goes off and does something else. As you follow the breath, what you begin to see is the mind's constant inner movement or dialogue.

How can you train the mind in the midst of this? In meditation, the first basic instruction is that each time you become aware that you have gone off into thinking or planning or remembering, you let go of the thought and return to the breath. So each time you drift away, return to feel the next in-breath or the next out-breath. If it helps, as you breathe you can say in the background softly, "in" during the in-breath and "out" during the out-breath. But let those words be only 5% of your attention, and let the other 95% be your awareness resting on your breath. The guided meditation included in this set is designed to help you with this basic process of becoming aware of your breath and then remaining in that awareness.

This first session of meditation practice is a beginning like the beginning of any art form. Like any other art form, the art of meditation takes some time to practice. Saint Francis de Sales said that what was necessary for a contemplative life was "a cup of understanding, a barrel of love, and an ocean of patience." This patience is also the willingness to come back again and again to the present moment in your meditation practice.

Training to work with the breath is a bit like training a puppy. You pick the puppy up and you set it down on a piece of paper and you tell it to stay. But does it stay? Not a chance. Like the mind, it gets up and runs around. So you pick it up and you put it back on the paper and tell it to stay again. After enough times of carrying it back and telling it to stay, the puppy begins to figure it out.

We are a little slower than puppies in this regard, but it is still possible for us to train the mind. Just like when the puppy pees in a corner, we can clean up the mess the mind makes and bring it back to the breath. The actual practice of meditation is the process of becoming mindful of the fact that you have strayed and then bringing your attention back to the breath and bringing the body and mind back together in the present moment. By doing it over and over again, your meditation practice begins to train you how to stay in the here and now wherever you happen to be.

Now if you have ever trained a puppy, you know it is not a great idea to beat the puppy when it strays. It is the same for us. When you realize that you are experiencing judgmental thoughts like "I cannot do this" or "I'm not doing it right," and you begin beating yourself up about it, that does not help at all. You just pick the puppy up gently, and bring it back to the next breath. You try to stay present for the next couple of breaths. It is that simple. Gradually, you will begin to connect with the breath.

Some common questions that come up for people during their first meditation sessions have to do with the different qualities of their breathing. People might feel that there is a sense of tightness in their breathing, as if their breath becomes artificial when they pay attention to it. This experience is quite common, and it is important to simply relax and try to let the breath move easily. If there is still a feeling of tightness, just let the tightness be there with an easy mind and a light heart.

Sometimes people also notice that their breath gets very soft, and they wonder if they should speed it up or make it stronger so they can feel it more easily. But the practice is to refine your attention so that you can listen more deeply and feel what is naturally in your body. So if you feel that your breath is soft, try to let your attention match the softness of your breath and to notice its beginning, its end, and the space between breaths — to become aware of the breath as it moves in your body.

Another universal experience that people notice is that their minds wander a hundred or a thousand times in ten minutes. It is natural that the mind wanders — it has been doing it for your entire life, and it is part of what all minds do. The art of meditation is to see the wandering of the mind and to acknowledge it in the moment, and then to return to your breathing. It does not matter how many times your mind wanders as long as you always bring it back to the breath. In some ways meditation is a remembering, or a self-remembering. It is a process of waking up, of being present with the breath or the body, and then a forgetting. Some people forget by having a lot of thoughts, whether they are creative thoughts, or problem solving, or memories, or whatever. Then after a while they wake up and realize their minds have drifted off, and then they wake up and remember, "Oh yes, I'm meditating." Then they reestablish their attention. Part of the process is nourishing or strengthening this capacity to wake up. While you are asleep, or when you have forgotten, there is not much you can do. But in the moment when you wake up, you remember to be present again. You can say to yourself, "Let me feel the breath, let me be aware of what is in this moment, what my body experience is like." Gradually, as you do this, you will be able to be present longer and longer, and it will happen more and more often—until you start to live more in the present moment and less and less in the place of forgetfulness or fantasy or memory. It is not that thought and planning and remembering are bad—we would not be able to live without them—but they often take up 95% of our whole lives. We could live more fully with a lot less thinking.

CHAPTER
FIVE

Meditation 2:
Working with the Sensations in the Body

THE FOCUS of our second meditation will be to include whatever arises in your body, the difficult sensations as well as the pleasant sensations.

After settling yourself in your posture and working with your breath,
the next step is to expand your field of awareness or mindfulness to
include all of the energies and sensations in your body. During meditation you may experience at different times a variety of sensations, such
as ease, tightness, pleasure, itching, and sometimes pain. All of these
sensations can be included in your meditation with the same kind of
attention and respect that we have begun to develop for the breath.

As you sit still, your body naturally begins to open. In its opening,
you often feel the things that the busyness of your life has kept
you from noticing. So at first you may experience unaccustomed

sensations solely because you are not used to sitting still. More deeply than that, you will sometimes feel tension in your shoulders, or jaw, or back, or belly, or some other part of your body. The reason for this is that as you sit and become still, the areas of tension that you carry and accumulate in your life are revealed to you. So as you are sitting and feeling the rhythm of your breath, all of a sudden certain places may become painful or warm or tight. What is necessary is to allow the opening of the body—whether it is painful or pleasurable—to be witnessed in the same spirit of attention that we give to the breath. When we can do this, whatever happens in our bodies will not be a problem, but rather a deep healing, even if it at first seems painful.

When the tension that we carry first opens, it will often show us all the conflict or pain or difficulty that we have stored in our bodies. When we pay attention to the tension with gentle awareness, it will gradually open and release. The central principle in allowing the body to be a part of meditation is to receive what arises for you with the same quality of presence or awareness that you have learned to experience with the breath.

There is a story about how Saint Francis would put his hand on the furrowed brow of a troubled person or even an animal, and with the kindness of his touch, remind them of their own inner beauty. Any energies that arise within us during meditation—whether they are tension, or pain, or pleasure, or difficulty—should be received with the same kindness that Saint Francis had when he put his hand on the brow of a troubled creature.

When you experience any bodily sensation during meditation, the practice is to name it to yourself softly, such as "tingling, tingling,

tingling," or "tension, tension, tension." As you do so, you give it space to open, and you also notice how the body itself wants to change and flow and move. So if you experience itching, instead of immediately scratching the itch, you can simply note "itching, itching, itching." Maybe for the first time in your life you can acknowledge the itch and feel what it is like and give it space to tingle and itch for some time without scratching it. Then you will also notice how it eventually passes away. This is true of every body sensation—whether it is coolness, or warmth, or tension, or pain.

As you pay attention to the opening of your body in meditation, it is also important that you do not decide intellectually what it is supposed to be like. Your meditation will open like a flower does, each aspect in its own time.

As you sit, you will discover that there are three kinds of painful sensations that can arise for you. The first is the signal that something is wrong, like your hand feels as if it is on fire. This is usually because you are in an uncomfortable position and your body is telling you to change the way that you are sitting. That is pretty infrequent, but once in a while you get that kind of sensation.

The second kind of painful sensation comes from sitting in an unaccustomed posture. A common experience is to get pins and needles and tingles in your legs. These kinds of sensations often occur when you are not used to sitting still or sitting cross-legged. It also takes a while for you to feel comfortable when you are keeping your back straight and unsupported. You can experiment by continuing to sit in order to feel what those pins and needles are like and let that be part of your meditation, and you can learn how to sit with something even that intense.

But if it seems too much to focus on at the time, then just simply change your posture and come back to your breath in a natural way. It is useful to experiment with posture. If you have a constant and fair amount of back pain of a certain kind when you are sitting, try to change your posture so that you can sit more comfortably. There is enough pain and difficulty in life without manufacturing more.

The third and most frequent type of pain includes every other uncomfortable sensation that comes with having a body. Sometimes when you are meditating, your shoulders will hurt, or your jaw will hurt, or your stomach will hurt. Often when you try to be quiet and these places start to hurt, it is because these areas have been tight all day long. We all have places where we stash our tension, and many people are even aware that they tend to clench their jaws or their shoulders—each time we experience stress or difficulty, areas in our bodies tighten in certain ways that lock in tension or pain.

So if you pay attention to these areas as you sit, you will allow them to open and sometimes even release that tension. It is not that you are supposed to get rid of the tension necessarily, but its important to bring it into consciousness. It means that you are actually beginning to feel your own body. Then over some time, it often begins to open on its own.

The goal is not to sit without pain. During some sittings you might have pleasure and bliss, and in others you might have pain. In meditation, as in life, you will usually get about an equal measure of pleasure and pain. So it is not that we try and minimize, or get rid of, or ignore, or run away from pain, because then you will have to spend half of your life running away. It is more useful to learn how to relate to all of it—the pleasure and the pain—with compassion, tenderness, mercy, and understanding.

As you pay attention to your body, it is important to focus not on how you think it should feel, but on what the sensations actually feel like. You can learn to feel pain and realize that it is not going to kill you. Maybe you have never let yourself fully feel pain before. Is it tingly? Does it feel like pinpricks? Is it fiery? Does it throb?

But you do not want to turn your meditation into a struggle with the sensations in your body. So if there is something opening in your body, you can give it attention as best you can, and if it becomes a struggle, then you can just release it and go back to your breathing. Be aware of the sensation for a while, and then return to your breathing. Perhaps you will be able to go back to the sensation in an easier way later on.

When you pay attention to the sensations in your body, they will invariably do one of three things: they will go away, they will stay the same, or they will get worse. Your job is not to control them, but just to be with them and let them come and go in your awareness.

There may be even more powerful releases that cause your body to shake or parts of your body will move spontaneously. That can be frightening, as if you are losing control of yourself. Usually when you experience sensations like these, your mind will start to think about them so that you do not have to feel them and realize how out of control the body is. But if you really think about it, your body is never completely in your control. Just as you are not really breathing on your own, but rather that breathing is happening, your heart is also beating on its own, and your liver is functioning without any guidance from you.

There are many other strange bodily sensations that will come and go in your meditations. You can feel light like you are floating, or heavy like you are made out of stone. Your breath can feel like it twists through your body. You can get flashes of coldness or heat, and all kinds of other things. The sensations that you will experience during meditation will sometimes be pleasant. Sometimes it will feel like there is a tingling or a thrill or some rapture happening inside your body that is out of your control. If you are not used to these kinds of feelings, they can be scary.

Physical sensations are usually the side effects that happen spontaneously as your body begins to open. Some people do not have them at all, and for some people they come more frequently. The most important thing is not the sensations themselves, but rather that you are able to find a centered place where you can touch a deeper level of your being. The layers of tension, and fear, and discomfort, and rapture are there, and you will encounter them, but they are part of the superficial layer of your life. What is important is that underneath them, you can connect with a place of centeredness and awareness that gives you strength and helps you to experience all the changes of your life.

It is also very helpful to know how to work with sounds in meditation, because lots of situations are inherently noisy. When you become aware that you are listening to some noise in your environment, you can include that listening in your awareness in the same way that you pay attention to the sensations in your body. You can simply feel the sound as it touches your ear, and you can note, if you wish, "hearing, hearing, hearing." You can let the sound be a wave, just like the breath is a wave. When the sound passes, then you can return naturally back to the breath.

I had a friend who lived in the city quite near a firehouse. At first he would get really upset because when he was meditating he'd be very peaceful, feeling his breath, and then suddenly the sirens would go off. But what he learned was that he could include the sirens in his meditation, so that when the sirens would go off, he would see if he was really present and mindful in that moment. After a while, he began wishing that the siren would come more often because it would always wake him up.

For this second meditation session, you will once again sit up straight and let your body hang in a relaxed fashion from your spine. Allow your eyes and face to be soft, and your shoulders and hands to be relaxed wherever they are comfortable. You will again use the breath as the center of your meditation, letting yourself feel the in-breath and the out-breath, noting the coolness, the swirls, the tingling, the itching, the pressure, the movement in your chest or your belly, whatever you experience wherever you experience it. These will be the center of your meditation.

However, as you sit and feel the breath, if there should arise any strong body sensation—tingling, or itching, or a fly on your nose, or a pain in your knee, or tension in your shoulders, or heat or cold, or any of the other energies of the body—let go of the breath and bring your attention to feel them fully. Receive them with awareness and kindness and give them a name. For instance, you could name the sensation "hot, hot, hot," or "itching, itching, itching," or "tingling, tingling," or "pain," or "pins and needles," or whatever it is. As you name your sensations, feel them as carefully as you can, paying attention to them as they change in a very relaxed way, even if they are difficult at first. Then when they pass away, go back to the next breath.

In this meditation you will alternate between feeling your breath and paying attention to your bodily sensations when they become stronger than your breath. Just as you notice your breath and allow it to rise naturally while noticing its beginning, middle, and end, you will receive any sensations or energy in the body fully and with the same mindfulness and kindness that you feel with the breath. In this way, you will come back to the breath or the body whenever the mind wanders, and just be there with them as you experience the moment.

CHAPTER
SIX

Meditation 3:
Working with Feelings and Emotions

THE RUSSIAN AUTHOR Alexander Solzhenitsyn has written that the line dividing good and evil cuts through the heart of every human being. It is not as if only others have anger, and fear, and hatred, and greed, and aggression. It is not someone else who is the cause of all the problems in the world, but it is the nature of all of us together. So it is a very important task in meditation to learn how to be with the most powerful energies of our own being and to find some compassion, mindfulness, and openness in the midst of all of our feelings and emotions.

By now you have probably noticed the play of moods or states of mind and feelings in the heart that change and very much determine your experience. So you sit and sometimes you are bored, or you are restless, or you are afraid, or you are happy, or you are in love, or you are depressed. You can see how when these states arise for us they can color the whole of our world. If you wake up and you are in a rotten mood—when you are angry and depressed and so forth—it almost does not matter who you see, there is something you will not like about them. Similarly if you are in love, you can have a car accident and say, "Oh, it is just my car, it is all right." It is obvious that the sensibility, feelings, and flavors of your mind and heart have a very powerful effect on what your life is like, almost more than the circumstances themselves.

When you experience your emotions directly, you may begin to weep or you might be sad, and after a while you can label it "sad, sad, sad" until it dissolves. Or sometimes, all of a sudden you realize that underneath that sadness is actually another emotion, like "lonely, lonely, lonely." Then you feel that for a little while until it goes away or it changes and you can go back to your breath.

Most people believe that if they could only get rid of all of their difficulties then they could really meditate. In fact, all of these difficulties are a very important part of your journey. We have so many opinions about what is good and what is not, but we really never know. Sometimes fully experiencing an emotion we think we should avoid—like anger or resentment—turns out to be the opening to the very lesson we need to learn. For instance, when you really study your anger deeply and learn to accept it without judgment, this can be the first step toward an understanding of it that begins a very deep movement toward forgiveness.

One afternoon I was meditating in a meadow and I was having kind of a "lah-dee-dah" meditation. My mind was doing creative things and planning, and every once in a while I was feeling the breath and just enjoying myself being somewhat quiet. Then, all of a sudden, a fly landed on my face. My first impulse was to brush the fly away because it tickled and was unpleasant, but then I thought, "Hey, I teach people to observe sensations like this, so I'll just stay with it." So I sat up a little straighter and I was just feeling the sensations— "itching, itching, tingling"—until the fly moved to the edge of my nose. My nostril was probably moist and it was a hot day, and the fly probably was attracted to the moisture. So I took a breath and decided to stay with the sensations. Then I began to feel fear that I might accidentally inhale the fly or it might climb up inside my nose and get caught in there. I began to feel my belly quiver and I watched the fear rise with these tiny footsteps on the edge of my nostril.

The fly stayed for at least ten minutes, and what was interesting to me was that during those ten minutes I was not planning, I was not doing my taxes, there was nothing creative going on, and I was not worrying about anything else. In fact, there was nothing else in the universe except for those tiny footsteps. By the end of ten minutes, I was more present and centered and concentrated than if I had gone to a monastery for a month.

The first feeling that many people experience in meditation is desire, or the "wanting mind." It is sometimes called the "if only mind." You are sitting there, following your breath, and all of a sudden your mind says, "If only I had something to eat." Or, "If only it were warmer," or "If only it were cooler." "If only I had a nicer, more comfortable meditation cushion." The problem with the "wanting mind" is that even if you get what you think you want, it does not stop. It

says, "All right, I have got the nice car, but now I need more money."
It is always something that we do not have in the present moment—
something that we want to obtain in order to satisfy our longing.

The way to work with desire in meditation is the same way we worked
with body sensations. It is not very useful to suppress it, because when
you do it comes out in some other way. On the other hand, you do not
want to act on it either. If you are like me and you acted on all of your
desires, they would lock you up. So you do not want to suppress your
desires, and you also do not want to act all of them out.

What you can do is to begin to use your desire for insight and
understanding, and to learn from your desire how to find some freedom
in your relationship to it. So when desire arises, you can sit and name
it as "wanting, wanting," or "desire, desire." You can examine it in order
to feel what it is like. If it is hunger, is your belly hungry? Is your
tongue hungry? Or is your hunger in your mind? Is it in your heart?
Often when we are hungry it is really because our heart is lonely.

In meditation, perhaps for the first time in your life, you are not
going to try to fulfill your desire, but you are going to sit and feel it
and see its nature. You will watch it arise, you will feel what it is like
in your body, and you will name it. Eventually it will pass away, and
then you will see the next thing rise up. You will begin to see desire's
impermanent nature, and you will also realize that you do not have to
act on every thought or desire. You will learn that you can choose
from the many possibilities of how to respond to desire when it arises, and you can discover a new kind of freedom, where you do not
have to follow your desires, but can choose to behave in new ways in
response to your desires.

So what do you do when this wanting mind continues to tap you on the shoulder? First of all, you can recognize that whatever it is saying this time, it is always just the wanting mind. Seeing this you can name it, in the same way that you named your bodily sensations. Instead of getting up and opening the refrigerator door or whatever your desire is, you can note it as desire or wanting, and you can you remain sitting there and feel the hunger or the wanting or whatever it is, and you can name it "wanting, wanting, wanting" or "if only, if only, if only," and sense what its energy feels like. Then you have a choice: Will you get up? Sometimes getting up may be the right thing to do, and at other times you will recognize the qualities of the wanting mind and find a way not to have to follow it every time it arises.

As you acknowledge desire or wanting, you can begin to see that your mind acts a little like a child at Disneyland: "I want that candy and I want to go on that ride and I want that stuffed toy." Even when you are trying to meditate, your mind is still a lot like a child at Disneyland, desiring a whole series of things. One of your options is just to continue to sit and acknowledge it. You do not have to get angry with your mind; you can just see that it is doing what a mind does and you can find a place of rest in the midst of it.

So you are sitting and feeling your breath quite naturally, and all of a sudden your mind says, "I do not like this. I do not want that. I want that to go away. I hate that." You are beginning to feel the resistance of the mind, which is the opposite of the wanting mind. In the same way, we can bow to this great force in our lives. Here is the wanting mind, and now here comes its opposite—aversion, anger, or fear, the aspects of mind that judge or push away our experiences.

This includes judgment, which is also a kind of aversion: "That is bad. You are doing it wrong." Aversion and judgment also include fear: "I do not want to feel this. I do not like this." This also includes boredom. Boredom says, "I do not want to be here. I want some other experience than what God has provided for me in this moment." Essentially, all of these are states of resistance.

As you experienced with desire, it is difficult to work with aversion, fear, and judgment when you get caught in them. Usually you have mostly acted out your fears, angers, and judgments unconsciously, without understanding them. The key strategy to working with them in meditation is to begin to face them. When you feel them rise up, instead of acting on them or pushing them away, you can embrace them. So if you are angry, then just allow yourself to be angry, and you can sit and label the feeling as "angry, angry." Then you will note what anger feels like in the body, what its energy is like, how it changes your breath. It is common to experience it as heat, but you can continue to examine it further: Is it pleasant? Is it painful?

When you notice an emotion like anger rising, you might also try to identify the quality that is there just before the anger. Right before anger arises, there is often a sense of hurt or fear or loss. When you can feel that, you can notice how little compassion or kindness you have for ourself and others. When we feel fear or when we feel pain or when we feel hurt, our response is often anger, but what is most healing is to acknowledge the anger and to notice what causes it, and to hold that in our attention.

In a similar way, you can be aware of judgment. You are sitting and your mind wanders, and you say, "My mind shouldn't be wandering.

I should be staying with the breath. I'm not doing it right." Then you say, "Well, I shouldn't be judging myself either," which is just another judgment. So you say, "I shouldn't be judging that either." Pretty soon you have a whole string of judgments. So what do you do with judgment? You can sit there and bow to it too, and you say, "There is the judging mind. Everyone has one."

Fear is another emotion that many of us would like to avoid or that we believe we shouldn't be experiencing. There is a story told of Mulla Nasrudin in which he was bragging that he had once caused a whole tribe of Bedouins to run. His friend asked him how the Mullah alone had made a whole tribe of wild bloodthirsty Bedouins to run. Nasrudin said, "It was simple. I ran and they all ran after me." This is the way that fear works. The farther we run, the faster the fear comes to find us.

When you meditate and fear arises, you can use the same process you've already learned where you sit and note "fear, fear, fear." When you sit with fear and name it, sometimes you will begin to feel what it is like in your body. How does it affect your breathing? Does it make your mind bigger or smaller? Then one day you will be sitting and fear will arise, and you will feel it and recognize it and think, "Oh, this is fear, I recognize you. Welcome back." Then it is as if the fear becomes one of your friends.

Another common energy that arises in meditation is sleepiness. Sometimes you sit down and feel so sleepy that your head begins to nod. Sleepiness is caused by different things. Part of it is that we are so busy that when we sit down and get quiet, our body says, "I haven't had enough rest. I have been running around too much." When this happens, you can acknowledge the sleepiness as a reminder from your body that you need to give it more rest. What can you do when this kind of sleepiness is really strong? You can open your eyes or stand up and continue to meditate standing up or while you are walking.

Other times when you feel sleepy, it is not so much that you haven't had enough sleep but that your body becomes very quiet during meditation and it is not yet used to being both quiet and alert. In that case, you would do best to sit up straighter or let your eyes be open a little bit wider to bring more brightness into your meditation. You could also breathe a few breaths more deeply, and you can also acknowledge the sleepiness in the same way that you bow to judgment or anger or the wanting mind by saying, "Oh, here's sleepiness…sleepy, sleepy, sleepy," and sense what it feels like and what it does and how long it lasts. In some sittings, it comes like a fog for a time and then it passes away. At other times it can be very difficult, but that does not mean that you have to struggle with whatever's happening—you can understand that these are the natural energies of your mind and heart, and that they can be included in your practice.

Now the opposite of sleepiness is restlessness and worry, and you can investigate what restlessness feels like. We are conditioned so that when we feel restless, or lonely, or bored, what do we do? We get up and turn on the TV, or we call someone on the phone, or we distract ourselves somehow. So our whole lives are spent running away from certain basic states like loneliness, or boredom, or restlessness, or fear. In meditation, however, when restlessness arises, you just label it "restlessness, restlessness," and feel what it is like.

What can you do when the feeling of restlessness is really strong?

You can continue to sit and say, "Okay, kill me. I'll be the first meditator in history to die of restlessness." In that moment, when you are willing to remain sitting even though you feel you are going to die, the restlessness changes. What makes these states so powerful is our resistance to them. But the moment you accept them, they lose a lot of their power. It is the resistance to them that makes them so difficult.

Another common experience that arrives during meditation is doubt. "I cannot do this. It is too hard to sit still," or "My mind is always wandering." "I'm too young. I should wait until I'm older," or "I'm too old. I should have started when I was younger." You may decide that this is the wrong kind of meditation. All of these thoughts say, "I cannot be where I actually am. I need it to be different somehow." What can you do when you experience doubt? You can simply bow to it, "Oh, there is the doubting mind. Everyone has it." You can watch the doubting mind as it comes and goes.

There are actually two kinds of doubt. There is the small doubt of "I cannot do it, it is too hard, it is the wrong day," and so forth. But there is also something called the "great doubt," which is the deeper questioning of who you are and questioning the nature of your heart and mind and consciousness. This is the doubt that brings us to realization or understanding.

As you sit, you will experience not only these difficulties, but also feelings of love, happiness, bliss, and rapture, and you can name these as well: "Love, happiness, bliss, rapture." The point is not to suppress them, but to open to what is there with awareness, with wisdom, and with kindness. We have cut ourselves off from so much in life, and we begin to understand this through the process of meditation and paying attention.

Now, one thing that you will notice when you are labeling the moods and emotions as they come is that they do not last very long. Thoughts come quickly. Thoughts generally last just a few seconds. Body sensations tend to be a little slower. Moods are in the middle. For the most part, there are about two or three different feelings per minute. If you are labeling your feelings, you will notice that a feeling will rarely last long enough to label it fifteen times before another feeling will arise.

Another kind of question that comes up is, "What if the feelings are really strong?" You are sitting and sadness comes up, and all of the sudden the grief that many of us have carried for years rises and you weep for a long time. The answer is that this, too, is fine. Sometimes the theme of meditation is sleepiness; sometimes it is tears and sorrow; sometimes it is joy. Whatever it is, let the feelings come and go as they will, and that will be your meditation. Sometimes the clouds need to weep themselves to their end, a poet said, in order for us to have the clear sky shine out from behind them. So do not be afraid of whatever feelings arise in meditation. Let them be a part of your practice. My teacher said that if you haven't wept deeply, you probably haven't meditated for very long.

For our third meditation, once again first sit in a way where your body is comfortable, erect, and stable. Let your eyes close, or leave them slightly open but downcast. In this meditation you will continue to work with the breath as your central object of attention, feeling as carefully as you can the actual sensations of the breath. When your body sensations are strong, you can name them as itching, tingling, hot, cold, pain, or whatever. When sounds arise and interrupt you—

like a loud car or someone coughing—then you can note those as "hearing, hearing." It is important not to create a story about whether they are good or bad noises but just to note the act of hearing until the noises, pass away and you can return to the breath. During this meditation we will see if we can also recognize the arrival of any strong moods or feelings like love, desire, anger, contentment, restlessness, doubt, or bliss. When you notice the arrival of any strong moods, let go of the breath and feel them as fully as you can. Experience what the individual emotions and feelings are like—such as wanting, rapture, or fear—and name them softly as long as they are present. Try to stay with them as long as they are there. Then, when the feeling passes, return to the next breath. When one mood passes, try to be aware of the next feeling that is present—peaceful might turn into calm, or sadness might turn into fear. Through it all, try to remain centered with your breath, your body, any sounds you become conscious of, and the movements of your heart.

CHAPTER
SEVEN

Meditation 4:
Witnessing Your Thoughts

AS MEDITATION OPENS further, people often say, "I'm lost in thought so much of the time, what should I do?" We have learned that the moods of wanting, restlessness, doubting, fear, or aversion will arise and pass, and we can bow to them and acknowledge them as part of the meditation. In the same way, there will be the movement of mind—or the "thought factory," I call it—telling stories and spinning out plans, memories, and fantasies. The simple task of meditation is to acknowledge that the thought factory is planning or remembering or whatever it is doing this time. Usually, when we acknowledge it with a single word or two as "planning, planning, planning," or whatever, it dissolves. Then you can come back to your next breath.

Sometimes we catch ourselves reliving something that happened to us in the past. There is a story told of the holy fool Mulla Nasrudin, who one day went into the bank to cash a check and was asked, "Could you please identify yourself?" So he reached into his pocket and pulled out a small mirror and looked into it and said, "Yep, that is me all right." That is a lot of what your mind does in meditation. It recapitulates the past. It tells us its stories of what happened to us in the past and imagines what will happen in the future. After a while you can get tired of those stories about the future and the past, but the idea is not to judge them. Instead, try to see that the stories aren't real— that each is a story that we insist on telling ourselves for a variety of reasons, but it is not what is happening in the moment. So we acknowledge the story as "remembering" or "planning," and return to the breath.

It ultimately does not matter how often you go away or how long your thoughts last because that is not really very much in your control. What matters is the magic moment when you wake up and realize, "Oh, I have been thinking." Whether it happens five seconds or five minutes later, that is the moment that makes a difference, because that moment gives you the choice to continue to be lost in thought or to come back again to the present moment. The act of returning is the training for awakening, for living in the present moment in a mindful way.

What about stories that repeat themselves over and over again? There are some stories that are like the Top Ten tunes in meditation. You are sitting there, and the record starts playing, telling the same story over and over again. Generally, if there is a thought that comes back to you over and over again, you can name it for whatever it is, such as "planning" or "remembering." If it keeps coming back, it is often a signal that something wants to be felt or accepted. So if the thought keeps returning again and again, there is maybe a loss that needs to be acknowledged, or a love that wants to be accepted, or some creativity that wants to be recognized and honored in some way.

You will also experience what I call "creativity attacks"— which is to say that when you become quiet, some deeper levels of reflection or understanding or dormant things that want to be expressed or understood will arise. Sometimes you can spend a little bit of time with these insights, but it is not a very good habit to form because it is easy to fill the mind. It is more useful to let the mind stay empty or to just let go of everything, including these powerful insights. There will be a lot of time when you are not meditating that you can spend with these insights. It is natural that they should sometimes arise during meditation, but instead of focusing on them, it is best to remember that you sat with the intention to meditate. You can say to yourself that when the meditation is over maybe you will think about these ideas some more, but right now you will continue with your meditation.

Thoughts are your associations to things. If you feel an itch, or you hear the sound of the rain, or there is a pain in your knee, those are all direct sensations. That is just an itch, or a sound, or a pain. But then as soon as the pain comes in, you think, "I wonder how much longer this will last?" Or you hear the rain and you think, "Gee, I wonder if it is going to rain tomorrow?" Or you feel the itch, and you say, "I didn't think there were any mosquitoes in here. I wonder what is making this itch?" First there was the direct sensation, and then there was the thought.

When you try to identify your thoughts in meditation, sometimes they will not come into consciousness right away. Or they might become very quiet. But if you wait patiently, all of a sudden a thought will say, "Gee, it is getting really quiet in here, isn't it?" Or they sneak up from behind and pretend they are not really thoughts. You will think things like, "There haven't been many thoughts, have there?" One problem is that we often tend to identify so directly with our thoughts that sometimes meditation is the first time you might actually be able to really listen to this inner stream.

After a while you begin to learn about your own style of thinking. Some people have almost all pictures and very few words. Others have both pictures and words, sometimes synchronized together, or sometimes the pictures will be more memories, or dream pictures, or other things, while the words will be planning, and they'll serve different functions. Some people have almost all words and very rarely have pictures.

You will discover that it is possible not only to become aware of the breath, or the body sensations, or the sounds, but also to become aware of this inner stream of images, and pictures, and words that for the most part are quite unexamined. One of the key insights in meditation is simply the nature of how your own mind is operating, and that there are possibilities of how you can relate to it. The first thing to do is to simply acknowledge how much time is spent lost in thought. One possible reaction to that is to take it very seriously and believe all of our thoughts and moods and so forth. Generally speaking, that leads to a lot of complexity and suffering. Another possibility is to listen from some place in our hearts that isn't in the mind, but which listens with a greater sense of spaciousness, or wisdom, or understanding, and then responds to things rather than being caught up in them.

In the fourth meditation session, again find a posture where you can sit comfortably and erect. When we begin, first go back to your breath, using that as the center of your meditation. Really listen to it and see if you can feel its beginning, middle, and end. Is the breath short, or long, or soft? As you pay attention to the breath, if body sensations, or sounds, or moods become quite strong, drop the breath and name them, giving them the same mindful attention you gave to the breath.

In addition, during this meditation we will include the field of thought. So as you follow the breath, if thinking arises and it is quite strong and it entangles you—whether it appears as a series of pictures or words, or as a memory or planning—then name it as "thinking." You might also note it as "planning, planning," or "remembering, remembering."

If it is a very charged or strong thought, you may note, "thinking, thinking," and it may continue. If that is so, then you can keep noting it softly— "remembering, remembering," or "planning, planning"—until it dissolves, and it will. Then you can go back to the breath. Just be aware of what is present without trying to change it, noticing with a gentle, careful attention.

Sometimes people are confused by the naming process. It sometimes seems too hard to name all the feelings and thoughts. "Was that a plan or a memory?" "Is this sadness or sorrow?" If it seems too complicated, keep the names very simple. You can either drop them or just note "feeling, feeling, feeling," or "thinking, thinking, thinking." The naming is an aid to help us to be simply aware of whatever is happening. You can use it if it serves you, and if it does not, you can just let your awareness be with whatever is present.

By this point in our meditation practice, our awareness has opened from the breath and the posture of the body to include the energies and the physical sensations within us. We have also learned to include the sounds that might arise around us, as well as the thoughts and images and stories that our mind creates. In this way, we open the meditation to all the music of life, to the dance of the energies we experience when we sit. We use the breath in the center of it as a way to still ourselves and become peaceful, and then we use that awareness to meet whatever arises with kindness and acceptance. In this way, whatever comes to us can be part of our meditation.

CHAPTER
EIGHT

Meditation 5:
Forgiveness Meditation

IN ADDITION TO THE MINDFULNESS practices where we have worked with the breath and the body, with the heart and the mind, there are also two complementary practices known as forgiveness and lovingkindness.

Forgiveness is one of the key arts of the spiritual life because when we forgive others, we are able to release the past and start life anew. Without forgiveness, we are always left with "who did what to whom," repeating the cycle over and over.

When I was with one of my teachers in a Cambodian refugee camp after the great holocaust in Cambodia, he set up a temple in the midst of the camp, even though he was warned by the Khmer Rouge not to do so. In fact, people were told that if they came to the temple when it opened, they would be killed. Nevertheless, 25,000 people gathered in the center square the day he rang the bell to open the temple. As he performed the ancient chants that had been central to their spiritual lives until the revolution, the people began to weep. When it was time to teach, all he did was to recite a simple phrase in Cambodian and Sanskrit that comes from the time of the Buddha which says, "Hatred never ceases by hatred, but by love alone is healed." These people, who had as much reason to want revenge as anyone in history and who had known as much sorrow as anyone I have ever seen, began to chant along with him. Somehow, as these people chanted, I could feel that the truth that they were chanting was even greater than their sorrow. This is the possibility of forgiveness that each human being holds in his or her own heart.

Forgiveness is not about condoning what happened. When you offer forgiveness, you can also say that what happened was wrong and that you will never allow it to happen again—that you would even put your own body in the way of letting such harm come to another person in the future. But forgiveness is the act of not putting anyone out of your heart, even those who are acting out of deep ignorance or out of confusion and pain. Forgiveness is also a matter of letting go of the past and knowing that, even though something was wrong, the way to go forward is to start over.

It is also important to understand that the practice of forgiveness is a practice, which means you might do it fifty or a hundred or more times before achieving an authentic sense of forgiveness in your heart. Some part of the process may involve rage and outrage, and some of it will probably involve grief and sorrow. Sometimes what arises in this process is that for the first time we fully come to understand how much anger we still carry and how deep our pain is. One cannot just paper over this pain with spiritual platitudes about forgiveness and extending love to others.

In a way, sometimes forgiveness means simply that we choose not to carry the hate inside us any longer because we realize that it is poisoning us. There is a story told of an American ex-prisoner of war who met another ex-prisoner of war many years after the Vietnam War. One prisoner of war asked the other, "Have you forgiven your captors yet?" The second said, "No, never." The first POW looked at him and said, "Well, they still have you in prison then, don't they?" It's important to realize that the extension of forgiveness most powerfully affects the person who is offering it.

At first, sometimes people find that offering forgiveness feels artificial or unnatural. It is fine if that is the way it is for you; you can just do the meditation and be receptive to whatever happens. Sometimes you will even experience the opposite of compassion, such as anger or frustration or emptiness. If this is your experience, you should hold those feelings in lovingkindness.

There is a place in everyone that yearns to love, that longs to be safe, that wants to treat others and ourselves with respect. Sometimes that place is buried underneath layers of fear, old wounds, cynicism, and pain that we have used to protect ourselves from injury.

So once again make yourself comfortable, let your eyes close gently, and come back to the breath. Let your attention be soft enough that you can feel the slightest movement your breath makes.

First you ask forgiveness for yourself for when you have hurt or harmed anyone in thought, word, or deed, knowingly or unknowing—and we all have. We all at times act unskillfully out of our own pain and fear. Allow these instances where you have harmed others to come into your mind and heart and ask forgiveness.

Then ask forgiveness for the ways you have hurt and harmed yourself out of fear, pain, ignorance, neglect, and dishonesty. Let the images of all of the ways you have hurt or harmed yourself come into your awareness and ask for forgiveness.

Finally, let the wounds and sorrows you have suffered at the hands of others come into your awareness. Realize that you have been wounded and hurt by others out of their fear, pain, and confusion. Feel the places in your heart where you hold resentment and touch them with kindness and forgiveness, and see if it is time to let go. Then, to the extent that you can at this time, extend forgiveness to those who have hurt or harmed you—knowingly or unknowing—in thought, word, or deed.

CHAPTER
NINE

Meditation 6:
Lovingkindness Meditation

LOVINGKINDNESS IS AN ANCIENT PRACTICE in which we con-
sciously direct the intention of our hearts to ourselves, and then to our
loved ones, and then extend it to all of the sentient beings in the world.

Mahatma Gandhi once said, "I believe in the essential unity of all
beings, and so I understand deeply that if one person gains spiritual-
ly, the whole world gains. If one person falls, the whole world falls to
that extent." Thus to wish others well or to send loving thoughts and
prayers to another is not simply a rote or automatic activity. The
practice is based on the effect our thoughts and feelings and actions
have on the world around us. Each of us participates in the ten thousand joys and ten thousand sorrows of our lives. We all have sorrows

enough to make anyone weep to hear them. Everyone also experiences enough beauty to fill anyone with joy. So by practicing the lovingkindness we connect our hearts to all of those around us.

There is a true story of two young children that illustrates this quality of lovingkindness. An eight-year-old girl was quite sick from a rare blood disease, and they searched all over for a donor and found that only her six-year-old brother could save her life. So the doctor and mother asked the boy if he would be willing to give his blood to help his sister. The boy asked for some time to think about it, and after two or three days, he went to his mother and said, "I'm ready to talk about it now." He agreed to do it. So the family went together to the doctor's clinic and the doctor laid one cot next to the other so that they could see each other while a bottle of blood was taken from the young boy's arm and put into his weak sister's body. When the boy saw the life coming back into his sister, he called to the doctor and whispered a question into his ear so his sister could not hear it. He said, "Doctor, will I begin to die right away?" He had not understood that when you give your blood to help another it is only part of your blood, and that is why it had taken him two or three days to think over whether he was willing to die to save his sister.

This is the basis for the meditation of lovingkindness. When you hear that story, perhaps you can remember that place in yourself that has so deeply loved another that you would give even your own life for them.

There was a study done on prayer groups several years ago by the chief surgeon at the largest medical center in San Francisco. Without anyone being aware of it, half of 250 patients were assigned to prayer groups that prayed for their well-being, and the other 250 patients had no one praying for them. When the study was over and the statistics were written up, the results were rather astonishing. The 250 people who were chosen at random to be prayed for left the hospital on the average of five days earlier, had fewer infections, fewer pulmonary problems, and healed more quickly from a variety of illnesses than the other group. This has been reported in a scientific journal, and most of the other physicians that I have talked to simply do not know what to make of it. But I do, and you do, too, because we know that who we are affects the world more than anything else.

Lovingkindness meditation is in essence a complement to the vipassana meditation we have been practicing. You can practice lovingkindness meditation at the beginning of a meditation session to soften yourself up, or you can do it at the end of your practice as a way of extending the spirit of kindness in your meditation. If the practice feels artificial or mechanical, you can experiment until you find words or phrases that make it work better for you. Some people find that it just isn't right for them, which does not mean they are not loving. If this is the case for you, just be loving enough to yourself to let it go and return to your breath or your next body sensation.

For most people, however, it is an exercise that, when worked with regularly, they find that they can gradually begin to develop and cultivate a stronger sensation of lovingkindness in their hearts. When you plant lovingkindness in the garden of your heart and continue to regularly nourish and fertilize it, it will begin to spread and grow.

Another nice thing about lovingkindness meditation is that you can do it anywhere and anytime. You can do it walking down the street: "May this person be happy, and may this person be filled with lovingkindness." Pretty soon, you can feel love for all of the people you pass on the street or in traffic. You can do it on the bus, and you can do it on an airplane.

Once again, you will begin by finding a comfortable place to sit and letting your eyes close gently, and allowing your body and breath to be soft. Then you will bring your attention into the area of the heart. See if you can feel your heart and breath together, as if you could breathe into and out of your heart. Feel your breath as if it comes in and out right there at your heart center.

Traditionally, lovingkindness meditation begins by directing lovingkindness towards yourself, because if there are things that you hate or you cannot accept in yourself, it is very hard to be loving of those things in others.

The next step is to begin to feel compassion for your struggles and sorrows. Everyone in the world experiences these very same pains and sorrows. So we try to embrace our sorrows with an open heart and with compassion and lovingkindness.

Next, try to cultivate a sense of who you were as a child and a sense of how children naturally elicit love in those around them—they do not have to do anything in order to earn their love. Then hold that image of yourself as a child in your open heart and try to open your heart to include all of the experiences of your body, all of your feelings, all of your moods and thoughts in this spirit of lovingkindness.

Then think of someone you love, someone for whom you naturally feel compassion. You know that they must suffer and struggle as you do, and you want to help them, you want them to be filled with lovingkindness and peace. Ask that their hearts be open and happy.

Then open your heart a little wider in order to include other loved ones into your heart, and wish that they will also be happy and that their hearts will remain open and be filled with lovingkindness and peace.

Then open your heart even further, large enough to let in all of your friends and the people you love. May they all be happy. May they be filled with lovingkindness.

Then try to make your heart even larger, large enough to fill the entire room, until it becomes a field of lovingkindness, large enough to hold all of the ten thousand joys and ten thousand sorrows that make up every human life.

Then feel your heart grow even larger than the room that you're in, expanding in every direction—in front of you and behind you, to the left and to the right, above and below you. Let your heart become large enough to hold your neighborhood, your city, your state, and the whole world, as if you could cover the Earth with feelings of lovingkindness. Picture the Earth and take it into your arms and your heart—all of the oceans and continents and the multitude of beings, whales and fishes and birds and insects and trees, jungles and deserts and everyone on the planet—until you can hold the whole Earth in the heart of lovingkindness and compassion.

Finally, ask that all beings be touched by the heart of lovingkindness; that all beings, those newly born, those in pleasure, those struggling in sorrow, those dying, those in between—that every creature and being be touched, and opened, and healed by the force of lovingkindness and compassion. May the power of your heart, of your goodness, of your love, bring that light to the world, and bring freedom to our lives and to those of all living beings.

CHAPTER
TEN

Meditation 7:
An Eating Meditation

WE SPEND A LOT OF TIME in our lives eating, buying food in supermarkets, growing it in our gardens, storing it away, taking it out, chopping it up, seasoning it, cooking it, serving it, eating with our friends, and then washing the dishes and putting all the food away. Most people eat two, three, or four times a day, and most of the time we do it all on automatic pilot. We can even go out to a restaurant and have a fabulous meal with nice conversation, a good glass of wine, and everything that makes for gourmet dining, and at the end of the meal still feel hungry. How can that be? Well, we are often so busy talking and looking around and having a good time that we never really have a chance to taste our meal.

Eating, like any other activity, can be turned into a meditation. If you do not want to get up right now and prepare a full meal, you can practice with something as simple as a few raisins.

First of all, if you want to practice an eating meditation in a formal way, you start by slowing everything down. You take your plate of food and put it in front of you. Some people like to say a little prayer or blessing for the food. One that many people use is a prayer of thanks for everything that was involved in bringing the food to your table. You can thank the Sun and the rain, and the people who grew it, and Mother Earth, and everything else you can think of. You can even give thanks to the earthworms that enriched the soil and the bees that helped to pollinate the vegetables. It is a fact that you could not live without the bees, and that your life also depends on the earthworms. Everything on Earth is interconnected.

Once you are finished with your blessing, then sit for sixty seconds with your plate in front of you and do nothing. You just sit there and relate to the silence. Maybe you notice the bodily sensation of hunger. Then look at your food and feel hunger, and realize that much of the world is in a constant state of hunger and desire. You can experience, perhaps for the first time, how difficult it is for you to sit with that feeling of hunger for even sixty seconds.

While you are doing this, you can examine how you experience hunger in your body. Is your belly hungry? Are your eyes hungry? Is your tongue hungry? What does hunger feel like? You can experience it and make your peace with it, and at the end of that sixty seconds you understand hunger a lot better. Or maybe other feelings come, and you can notice those as well. Maybe you hate raisins, so hatred arises. Label it "hatred," and experience your hatred for raisins fully in this moment.

Then, when you are ready, begin to eat, and do it slowly and mindfully, the same way you followed the breath or were aware of the other sensations in your body. First hold the raisins in your hand and really look at them. Try not to see them as raisins, because "raisins" is just a word. Instead, try to see them as their own individual forms, shapes, and colors.

As you continue to look at the raisins, you can become aware of their whole history. First, they grew on vines and became grapes, then they were harvested and left in the sun for a while. Then they were packaged and shipped, you bought them, and now you are about to eat them. You can realize that you are part of a larger web that involves the whole Earth. You are an animal, and this is something that was grown by the Earth, and now you are going to turn it into energy in your body, something that will help you remain alive.

Touch the raisins with your fingers. Try not to feel them as "raisins" but to directly experience whatever sensations you can. Do they feel sticky? Soft? Do they give way when you press into them? Are they cold, warm, neutral?

Then check in with your body. Can you feel yourself salivate? Notice how your body automatically begins to salivate when you experience hunger, without having to think about it.

When you are ready, bring them to your mouth. Slow the movement of your arm so that you can feel all of the sensations involved in even raising your hand to your mouth. Then, just as slowly, open your mouth and feel what that is like. Place the raisins on your tongue, but do not begin to chew them just yet. First examine what they feel like on your tongue, and then slowly close your mouth and lower your arm. When you are settled, close your eyes and begin to chew. Taste them and swallow the raisins mindfully. Then remain mindful even after you have swallowed. Can you feel the food go down your esophagus and into your stomach? Once you are done, slowly open your eyes.

When you eat an entire meal with this kind of mindfulness, it actually changes your relation to food and eating—you realize that a little goes a long way. Even with the raisins, you probably realized that there is a lot to just a couple of raisins. In fact some people call this the "vipassana diet"—the only rule is that you really pay attention when you eat.

One thing that people notice with the raisins is that the flavor does not last very long. You probably chewed them for a while, and then the flavor went away. You still had to keep chewing, but the last part of the chewing was not so flavorful. That is often the point where people reach out for a few more raisins. They will chew for a bit, not even ready to swallow yet, and the flavor kind of dies out, so they will put a couple more in their mouths.

Why do we do that? Because the flavor is sweet and it is pleasant. Then what do we experience next? Desire and grasping. We want more of that, and so we try to get the next hit even before we have swallowed the last one. In a mouthful of raisins, you can see the whole cycle talked about in Buddhist psychology—that life is an array of constantly changing sensations; some of them pleasant, some of them unpleasant, and some of them neutral. Our unconscious response is to grasp after the pleasant and to try to resist the unpleasant, so that we are always at war with the basic transience of our experience. We cannot really come to rest with things as they arise and depart.

When you practice mindfulness while eating raisins, you begin to learn something other than the usual habit of grasping and pushing away. You begin to notice not only the sweet, but also that it does not stay the same and eventually disappears. You can be aware of its absence, and you can be with whatever comes next as well—which is the essence of all meditation.

Another aspect of the eating meditation is that when you eat an entire meal in this state of mindfulness, you can try to identify the different voices that talk to you while you are eating. Most people can identify at least half a dozen voices. Your stomach may speak first, that it has had enough and is comfortable as it is. But then your tongue might say, "That stuff over there was really good, I want a little more of that." Your eyes might say, "Yeah, and we haven't even tried the dessert yet." Then some voice in your head might say, "No, you better stop—you are too fat as it is." Then your mother will come in and say that you are not finished until you have eaten everything on your plate. You will hear each of these different voices with their different opinions about how much or how little you should eat.

Some people do an eating meditation for one meal every week, or for one snack a day, where you eat an apple and make it a fifteen minute eating meditation. Most people find that learning how to occasionally eat in this way also greatly enhances their physical well being.

The point of this meditation is to make each of those voices conscious until you can see which ones you habitually follow, and then perhaps to learn how to begin listening to the other voices as well. The whole art of living wisely depends on our paying attention—and you can learn to pay attention to your experiences even when you are not sitting on your meditation cushion. And, since we all have several meals every day, practicing an eating meditation is another great opportunity for us to become conscious several times a day.

CHAPTER
ELEVEN

Meditation 8:
A Walking Meditation

ANOTHER MEDITATION you can do is a walking meditation. I recommend that at first you practice this meditation for fifteen to twenty minutes, so that you can get some sense of how it will work for you. For this meditation all you need is to find, either in your house or somewhere outdoors, a place where you can walk back and forth for about twenty to thirty steps in length. It is best if you practice this mostly in the same place so that you will not be distracted by the newness of your surroundings. This is not a nature walk — you will be concentrating on your walking, not your surroundings.

The first thing to do is to go that place and stand still. You will keep your eyes open and slightly downcast in this meditation. Feel your feet on the floor or on the ground. It does not matter if you are wearing shoes or not, just feel in contact with the earth. You can let your hands rest wherever they are most comfortable—most people let them hang at their sides. Spread your feet about shoulder-width apart.

Bring all of your attention to standing still. Notice whatever body sensations you are experiencing—if you are outside, you might feel a breeze, you might smell the scent of grass or flowers in the air. Feel the sensations in your limbs, like your shirt brushing against your shoulders and your elbows, or the stiffness or hardness in your feet and legs.

As you do this walking meditation, you will bring the attention you have learned to bring to your breath during sitting meditation to the act of walking. Begin by shifting your weight slowly onto your left foot. Feel what that is like. Now one leg is stiff, heavy, and hard; and the other is empty and light, and the knee is bending easily. You can even bring your heel off the floor, but not your toes. Then slowly shift your weight to the other side. Feel what that is like.

Take a tiny step with your left foot, just an inch or two forward. Notice both actions—lifting and placing. Now shift your weight forward onto your left foot. Take a tiny step with your right foot. Lifting, placing. Then feel your weight return to center. What is most important is to feel the steps themselves—the heaviness of one foot changed into lightness—and then to feel the movement in your leg, to feel it lowering and touching the sole of your foot to the ground, and the contact it makes as it gets stiff and heavy. Lifting, placing. Lifting, placing. It is similar to Tai Chi or a very slow, mindful dance. You can even say the words "lifting" and "placing" to yourself if it helps.

After you have gone about twenty steps, stop and center again. Then you turn around slowly, lifting and placing. Now you will return in the opposite direction. Continue to walk this way, back and forth, mindfully so that you are not on automatic pilot.

As you walk, if your mind wanders off and you catch yourself, just bring your attention back to what you are doing. Lifting, placing. If you have gone very far away in your thoughts, just acknowledge that you have been away and center yourself, and then go back to lifting and placing.

If you want to stop and look at something, you can stop and look at it. Be aware of seeing, and you can even label it as "seeing, seeing" or "appreciating" or whatever it is. Then when you are through, center yourself again and return to lifting and placing.

You can also experiment with what speed keeps you the most present, and you can vary your pace if you are sleepy or if walking slowly does not work for you. You should be walking at whatever speed helps to keep you the most aware.

Walking meditation is a particularly good practice for both our most ambitious days and those days when we feel easily distracted. When you bring your attention to walking back and forth in one place, you realize pretty quickly that the point is not to get anywhere, but to be where you already are. This, of course, is the essence of meditation.

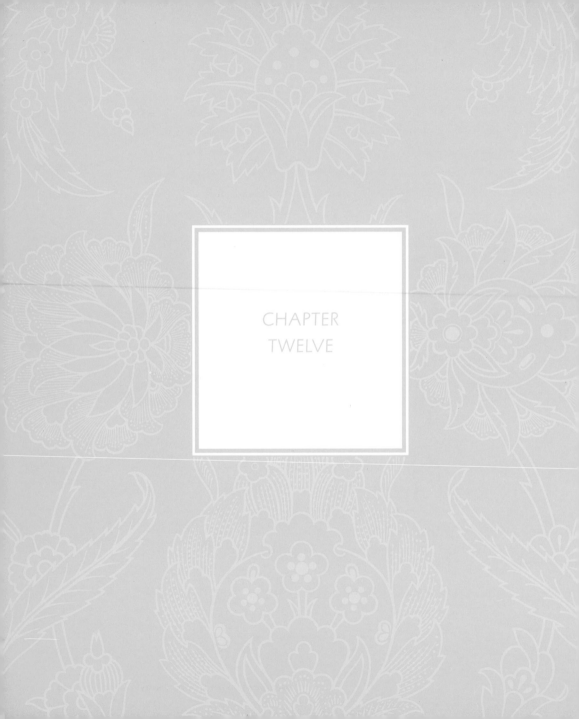

CHAPTER
TWELVE

Meditation and Social Responsibility

SOME PEOPLE THINK OF MEDITATION not as a practice that makes us more present, but as something that will lead us away from the world. If we become attached to solitude, that can lead us away from the world. But for a spiritual practice to be alive in your life, you have to be able to use it in the supermarket, or when you are driving, or when you are dealing with your family. We can go on periodic meditation retreats, but the larger purpose of meditation is to realize how we are a part of everything, and not try to escape from any aspect of our lives. An important aspect of our lives is our social responsibility.

I have heard compelling arguments for two very different points of view on our social responsibilities. From one perspective, it is essential for us to be engaged with the difficulties that surround us, especially the exploitation and injustices that are perpetrated all over the world. It seems that we are constantly either at war or preparing for war. For millions of people, war is not just an idea but a painful daily reality. As are starvation, and poverty, and disease, and all of the suffering in the world. Even in our very rich and affluent society, people are suffering in many ways. From that point of view, what is most important is what we do to end suffering and injustice. Is it possible to be aware of this and spend our time sitting in meditation?

But there is another point of view that is equally convincing, and that is that the best way to alleviate war and suffering is to learn the causes of them. For instance, what is the cause of starvation and wars and suffering? There is enough oil. There is enough food. There are enough resources on this planet. The cause of much of the suffering in the world is greed, and the cause of it is prejudice and hatred. We like our country, our family, and our religion, and we hate people of different religions, with different skin colors, with different customs. There is hoarding, grasping, greed, hatred, and ignorance. There have been hundreds of revolutions throughout history, and, although they've helped in some ways, in other ways the same kinds of problems keep happening again and again, because we haven't addressed the root of the problem.

The root of the problem is that everyone has to first discover the root of anger and hatred inside themselves before they can understand how it operates in the outside world. The solution to the problem is for everyone to learn how to be free of the fears and prejudices that arise in human hearts and minds. To do that, we have to learn how to see the world exactly as it is, and not be afraid of what is painful or to be seduced by what is pleasant. We have to discover how to keep our hearts open to everything we encounter and everyone we meet.

From this perspective, we do not need more oil or food or money or anything external, as much as we need people who understand how not to get caught in anger, fear, and prejudice. In this way, meditation is not a luxury or an escape from the world, but it is a deepening sense of our responsibility to learn how not to be caught by these forces. That is why, in our meditation practice, we first learn what this understanding means for us on the inside before we bring that understanding to our interactions with the economic, social, and political suffering in the world.

But there is also a very real danger that we could use meditation as a way of retreating from the world. There is a teaching in the Buddhist tradition called the "near enemies." For instance, the near enemy of love is attachment. It masquerades as love, it feels like love, but it is essentially different. When it says "I love you," it really means "I'm attached to you and I need you to make me whole." The near enemy of compassion is pity: "Oh, that poor person over there, they are suffering. I do not suffer like that." Pity keeps us separate from and superior to those for whom we believe we experience compassion.

The near enemy of equanimity, or a balanced mind, is indifference. It masquerades as equanimity because we feel that everything is fine. However what it really means is that we have no feelings for anyone else. Real equanimity arises when our hearts are open, and we experience everything that the world presents to us with balance, love, and understanding. We are not running away from the world at all; we are sitting down right in the middle of everything and paying attention to everything that is present—whether it is something pleasurable or something painful—and beginning to observe it, to learn from it, and to learn a wise way of relating to everything in our lives.

CHAPTER
THIRTEEN

How to Cultivate a Daily Meditation Practice

ONE OF THE MOST IMPORTANT aspects of meditation is to cultivate a daily practice. If you do, the first thing you will notice is that on Monday you might be able to be with your breath very well, but on Tuesday it will be a struggle, and on Wednesday it will be even worse than that. Then on Thursday it might be better again, but on Friday it could be completely frustrating.

It is important not to judge your meditations. Your job is to sit on the cushion or the chair and to accept and relate to whatever happens, which will always be solely a reflection of whatever state your mind and body are in at that moment. Even if you are frantic at the end of the day and you can sit and watch three breaths in the twenty minutes and the rest is a lot of thinking, do it anyway. Try not to have expectations. Just commit to practicing it as an exercise, and do not get discouraged by whatever happens. Remember that meditation practice is very much like learning how to play the piano. At first it amounts to little more than getting your fingers to work a series of exercises. Later, you may be able to forget about the exercise and hear the music behind it. We have all spent probably a hundred million moments of wandering mind in our lives already, so to try to change the wandering mental habit overnight is not very likely. Meditation works, but it takes perseverance and a gentle training of yourself.

Here are some suggestions to help you establish a daily meditation routine.

- Choose a time of day that works for you, and then try to meditate around that time every day.
- Accommodate your personal style. If you are a morning person, you may want to meditate shortly after rising. Others find it easier to sit in the afternoon, or in the evening.
- Find a quiet corner where you can practice every day. It can be anywhere, as long as you can remain relatively undisturbed during your meditation session. Use a chair, a cushion, or any support that best helps you maintain your meditative posture and awareness.
- Sit for fifteen minutes, half an hour, or longer each day. Even just five minutes a day will be beneficial, as long as you make the simple commitment during that time to feel your breath, and bring your awareness to your physical sensations, thoughts, and feelings.

- Depending on your inclination each day, use any of the meditations featured in this book, or any combination of them.

- You may find it helpful to place inspiring objects in your meditation space: an image, some incense, or possibly a book. You might want to read a short passage from a book before meditating. Many meditators light a candle to symbolize the illumination that is the gift of awareness.

- Seek out a meditation group. These can be found through churches, temples, Buddhist or Hindu groups, and various secular organizations. Joining such a group does not commit you to becoming a follower of any particular teaching; it simply surrounds your practice with the support of other meditators.

- Remember that meditation is not an accomplishment, but a lifelong practice. As you work with your breathing, bodily sensations, thoughts, and emotional energies, you will become more adept at remaining calm and curious in the midst of any life situation.

- Keep it simple. The point of vipassana meditation is not to have any particular experience, but to become aware of whatever experience you are having. An attitude of childlike openness will help you discover the truth of your life in the present moment.

The two vipassana meditation centers
cofounded by Jack Kornfield are:

Insight Meditation Society
1230 Pleasant St.
Barre, MA 01005
www.dharma.org/ims.htm
978-355-4378

Spirit Rock Meditation Center
PO Box 169
5000 Sir Francis Drake Blvd.
Woodacre, CA 94973
www.spiritrock.org
415-488-0164

About the Author

JACK KORNFIELD trained as a Buddhist monk in Southeast Asia. He is cofounder of the Insight Meditation Society in Barre, Massachusetts, and the Spirit Rock Meditation Center in Woodacre, California. His books include *Teachings of the Buddha; A Path with Heart; After the Ecstasy, the Laundry;* and *Living Dharma*. He also holds a Ph.D. in clinical psychology, and lives in northern California with his wife and daughter.

SOUNDS TRUE was founded in 1985 by Tami Simon, with a clear vision: to disseminate spiritual wisdom. Located in Boulder, Colorado, Sounds True publishes teaching programs that are designed to educate, uplift, and inspire. With more than 600 titles available, we work with many of the leading spiritual teachers, thinkers, healers, and visionary artists of our time.

For a free catalog, or for more information on audio and video teaching programs by Jack Kornfield, please contact Sounds True via the World Wide Web at www.soundstrue.com, call us toll free at 800-333-9185, or write

The Sounds True Catalog
PO Box 8010
Boulder, CO 80306

CD SESSIONS

1. Connecting with
the Breath 12:41

2. Working with the
Sensations in the Body 12:52

3. Working with Feelings
and Emotions 14:02

4. Witnessing Your
Thoughts 9:56

5. Forgiveness
Meditation 7:13

6. Lovingkindness
Meditation 10:50